THE PROFITABLE
CONTENT SYSTEM

THE ENTREPRENEUR'S GUIDE
TO CREATING WILDLY PROFITABLE
CONTENT WITHOUT BURNOUT

THE PROFITABLE CONTENT SYSTEM

THE ENTREPRENEUR'S GUIDE TO CREATING WILDLY PROFITABLE CONTENT WITHOUT BURNOUT

MEERA KOTHAND

WWW.MEERAKOTHAND.COM

CONTENTS

THE BIG, BOLD PROMISE

Content that directly drives sales...

It's a juicy thought, right?

Especially when your pain index related to creating content is skyrocket high...

When it feels like you're scrambling to fill your content pipeline week after week with little to show for it in terms of results...

No subscribers.

No brand authority.

No shares.

You're struggling to stay afloat with content creation and promotion and the eighty-seven tasks in between, like creating images or social media posts or tweets.

The reason most entrepreneurs get caught in the never-ending cycle of content scramble?

Their content system isn't set up to scale or help them grow without adding more stress and overwhelm to their days.

What I'm going to share with you here is not a long, drawn-out strategy.

Your content efforts CAN directly lead to sales, and you'll find out how in just a bit.

Now, what exactly do I define as content?

Content is all of the following:

- email
- social media posts
- content channels (YouTube, microblogging, blog posts, podcasts, etc.)
- infographics
- videos

- and more

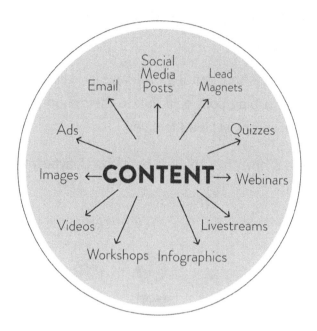

You can strategically create an array of content pieces that make your products and services fly off your virtual shelves.

But not in the way you think it should.

There are two camps of entrepreneurs when it comes to content and sales.

CAMP ONE

The first camp thinks of content and sales the wrong way.

They think that putting an image or call to action within a blog post or a link to their shop page is how content will lead to sales.

Here's how they think it happens (maybe you do too!):

Sure, there are people who do exactly this.

But these are exceptions rather than the norm.

A very tiny percentage of your website visitors will actually buy in this manner.

When you think that this is the only way content can drive sales, you're not actually understanding the purpose of your primary content channel.

Your primary content channel is the main platform you use to share content with your audience. It could also be one of your main channels of lead generation—your primary method of attracting subscribers onto your email list.

But doesn't it make sense to place an offer on your blog or YouTube channel or podcast?

Yes, but 96% of visitors to your site aren't ready to buy.[1]

Furthermore, in a survey by the Economist Group, 71% of those surveyed said that they have been put off by content because it seemed more like a sales pitch,[2] especially when they were there to look for more information.

Does this mean you can't sell?

Aren't you in business to sell?

Yes, and I'm not telling you to shy away from selling.

But a blog or your primary content channel (be it a YouTube channel or podcast) is a content medium you use at the **top of your funnel or at the beginning of your buyer's journey.**

It's a tool you use to attract new readers.

The role of this primary content channel is to provide answers to the questions your readers are asking...

To satisfy their doubts...

To build that first layer of trust.

So it doesn't make sense to push sales via your blog or primary content channels.

If I just spoke alien, don't worry. I'll talk about this in more detail later on in the book. But if you just did an eye roll at the mention of a funnel...

Or you're jaded with everything funnels because it didn't seem to wield any magical powers for your business like people said it would...

Or maybe you don't like the idea of squeezing your readers through a pipe...

That's fine!

But I do think the good ole funnel still serves some value in helping you understand the different people interacting with your brand at any one time.

It's also useful in helping you map your content to these different people because there's a direct link between how people seek out content and how they use that information to make an educated buying decision. We'll talk about this in detail in section 2.

So if you're in this first camp...

If your idea of a sales and content relationship is a link to your sales page or an image of your offer, then we're going to change that.

Note: I'm not referring here to content creators who use advertising and affiliate links to generate revenue. I'm referring to those who sell services, digital products, coaching, or memberships.

And by content channel, I'm not just talking about a blog. This could also be a podcast or YouTube channel. So swap my examples out for listeners or viewers if a YouTube channel or podcast is your primary content channel.

CAMP TWO

The second camp thinks of content and sales as distinctly separate categories.

Content is for attracting more traffic, while sales is for—just that—selling more digital products or landing more clients.

What's wrong with traffic, likes, or shares?

Nothing.

But these are purely vanity metrics.

You can give yourself a pat on the back for getting fifty thousand monthly visitors, but if you can't monetize that audience, then your content doesn't count.

Content, in a vacuum, can't do much to help your brand.

Can you get tons of traffic and still not see a single cent? YES.

Can you get likes and shares and still make only $4.57 from your site? YES.

Sure, social shares are a useful metric that tell you whether your content is popular. But popular content doesn't necessarily lead to sales.

The same goes for traffic.

A particular piece of content can drive a ton of traffic to your site, but if that traffic doesn't include people who have the ability and willingness to buy from you...

If that content isn't aligned with your business or offers you have—if it doesn't help the reader through their stage in the buyer's journey—then that piece of content doesn't help your business at all. Because you'll struggle to turn those visitors into leads, sales, and profits.

If you're doing it right, more readers to your site should translate to a bigger email list. A bigger email list should translate to more sales.

CONTENT IS NEVER THE END GAME

Content is always a means to an end.

Whether you're creating a blog post or an email series or an email course, you need to have a clear reason as to why you're doing so. You need to define the purpose and goal of that content even before you create it.

This was the basis of my first book, *The One Hour Content Plan,* which I published in 2017. It became an Amazon best seller within forty-eight hours of launching and to date has sold more than ten thousand copies worldwide.

In that book, I share this unhealthy obsession with wanting to fill a publishing queue and how you should move away from publishing content just for the sake of doing so. *The One Hour Content Plan* also gives you a framework of what intentional content looks like.

Intentional content is content that feeds your business goals. Most businesses get started with content because it's the "right" thing to do, but they're not able to articulate what their content goals are. That's why having a content strategy is critical.

Your content strategy is the actual engine that drives your content marketing (i.e., the process of coming up with content ideas, creating, publishing, and distributing the content).

There are six specific pins that drive your content strategy engine. You need to figure out all six to have a solid content strategy.

- **Content Foundation or Content GPS**
  - Your content categories and brand voice
- **Audience**
  - Your ideal reader persona: an accurate description of your ideal reader beyond

demographics. It should include psychographics as well as motivational factors that drive them.

- **Content Ideation**
  - The process of coming up with content ideas
  - A system to capture content ideas into a swipe file
- **Editorial Calendar**
  - The actual workflow of how to plan, manage, and publish content
- **Content Creation**
  - How to keep readers hooked on your content
  - Writing content that ranks for specific words or phrases that are relevant to your buyers and audience and which they seek out regularly
- **Content Maximizers**
  - How to amplify and supercharge your existing content

In *The One Hour Content Plan*, I specifically covered the EOG Method, content GPS, creating an audience persona, and content ideation. If you're just starting out in your business and don't have products and services yet, I highly recommend starting with *The One Hour Content Plan* first.

In this book though, I want to show you how to create content that *directly* drives sales via the

Profitable Content System. So if you already offer products or services, this book will be right up your alley.

The Profitable Content System is a profit-aligned method of content planning. It'll supercharge the content you create and tie it directly to revenue. So if you've been winging it with content or if you've not been taking note of whether you're getting any return on investment at all from your time spent on creating content, this method will change how you approach content and plan your business.

We'll break down each of the eight steps in the Profitable Content System in detail so that you can take advantage of this powerful method for your own business.

I'll also introduce you to a process that allows you to seamlessly integrate the Profitable Content System into your own system. You'll discover how to maximize your content and a simple SNAP Recipe to make your content relevant in today's age of content shock[3] where supply exceeds demand.

You'll see first-hand through case studies how the Profitable Content System can be applied across three different niches—beekeeping, design services, and visibility & PR.

What are some of the results you'll see by adopting the Profitable Content System?

1. Selling becomes a natural "next step"

I still see entrepreneurs showing up on their cart open date and announcing that their offer is for sale. You should create a conversation around the topic of your offer at least 3–4 weeks in advance of your cart open date. Because if you don't, then you're not engaging your audience...

You're not preparing them to buy from you...

You're not addressing questions or objections they may have prior to the sale. This is one of the biggest reasons launches flop. The Profitable Content System allows you to open a conversation with your audience before you ever send them to a sales page.

2. It makes your message stronger

The Profitable Content System focuses your content on a single subject at a time. This allows your audience to explore each topic in detail. It focuses their attention on your point of view of the topic and how your framework or process or methodology can get them the transformation they're looking for.

3. You build content-expert association

Even if your audience doesn't buy from you right away, you're still serving them with content that builds your authority and gets them to associate you as someone they can trust with the topic of your offer. And who knows? They may become a customer and brand advocate down the road!

Does this mean you are always selling to your audience?

Yes and no.

Selling isn't a bad thing.

At the same time, when you do it this way, it will not feel like selling at all.

If you dream of having a yearly plan for your content based around your products and services...

If you want to give your audience insanely valuable content that leads to your Stripe and PayPal accounts pinging with joy...

If you desperately desire a workflow that doesn't seem crazy overwhelming...

If you're ready to have the confidence that comes from knowing that every month will be a solid four- or five-figure month even when you do minimum viable promotions...

If you think your content does nothing for you and that it's a waste of time...

Then you could use the Profitable Content System!

If you're ready, let's go!

You can download the Profitable Content System Playbook and bonus resources at https://meera.tips/contentplaybook.

SECTION I

GRAVY — THAT WHICH FEEDS THE PROFITABLE CONTENT SYSTEM

Let's start this section with a question.

Whether your business is your own personal brand or a standalone brand, why did you start creating content?

Go ahead.

Think about your answer.

Hopefully you have a few different answers.

Maybe some of those answers are because you *thought* you had to do it...

Or because it's nice to have or because you saw others doing it.

By now you know that those aren't valid reasons.

As an entrepreneur or small business owner with products and services as part of your business model, you create content for **one main reason.**

You create content to handhold potential customers through the buyer's journey.

The buyer's journey is the process buyers go through to become aware of, consider and evaluate, and decide to purchase your offer. Your customer is going to be at one of these three stages in the buyer's journey.

In effect what you want to do is address their questions and educate them so that they can make the right decision. You want to convince them that your offer is the right solution.

There's a direct link between how people search and find information or content and how they use that information to make an educated buying decision. This is even more important today because the way your audience buy and the way they seek information has dramatically changed.

Sales teams used to be gatekeepers of information about a product or offer. You had to speak to a salesperson to find out about an offer. You had to call in for a catalogue or you'd get printed catalogues sent in the mail.

But now, we hardly ever need to go to a showroom or call to speak to a sales representative unless we want to.

Yet, we're far more informed and savvy consumers.

Think about how you buy.

You're met with a challenge or pain point.

You start to search for answers on this challenge or pain point—whether that's for a skin cream for postpregnancy acne or an ergonomic chair for your back pain.

You read reviews, compare products, or talk to your friends on social media.

You do this even before you hit a shop or are in any position to buy.

You research, compare, and decide who you want to buy from and when, all without leaving your home, in your own time without pressure.

This is what Google calls the "Zero Moment of Truth,"[4] or ZMOT—that moment when you start learning about a product or service you're thinking about trying or buying via social media or internet searches.

On average, 70% of the buying decision is made online before someone contacts a business for the first time.[5] This is when first impressions happen and the path to purchase often begins.

But how is this relevant to us doing business online?

Maybe you don't have a physical product...

Maybe you sell digital products like e-books or courses or coaching...

Maybe your offer name doesn't show up when you do a search online compared to the big brands or others selling popular physical products.

It doesn't matter.

You can and should still be a part of the Zero Moment of Truth.

And you do that by answering questions your audience has at each phase in the buyer's journey.

This is exactly what we're going to delve into in the next chapter.

CHAPTER 1

THE STAGE ×10 FRAMEWORK

How do you know if someone is ready to do business with you?

- They recognize they have a problem and are aware of what this problem is costing them.

- They have a desire for the "after"—of how things could be if they solved that problem or pain point.

- They discover that solutions exist.

- They understand what they should consider when choosing a solution.

- They are convinced that your solution is the right one for them and that their fears and assumptions are baseless—or at least can be managed.

Don't you check off all those boxes as well before you buy an online program, order a serum that clears acne scars in five days, or download a video app that promises to shorten your editing time by 80%?

But not everyone who lands on your blog, YouTube channel, or podcast for the first time is going to have the same level of awareness about the topic of your offer.

And people at different stages in the journey have different questions.

These different levels of awareness reflect their readiness to do business with you.

For instance, if you run a virtual assistant (VA) business, not everyone who comes to your site is ready to hire a VA on the next call. They may not yet be convinced. They may have a ton of questions from whether it's the right time to hire a VA, to whether they need a generalist VA or someone more specialized, to the types of tasks they can outsource to a VA. They may even be skeptical about the direct benefits a VA will have to their bottom line.

As a content creator, you want to be sure to serve your audience by addressing the questions they have at each phase in order to inch them to the next. You want to get them to a stage where they are ready to hire.

The same goes for digital products and coaching. Your offer solves a problem and gives your ideal buyer a transformation. But your prospective buyer will have a ton of questions about the problem that your offer solves.

Heck, some people may not even know they have a problem!

They may be seeking solutions for the **symptoms they're experiencing without seeing the underlying problem.**

Let's dig into this concept further.

If you're familiar with my content, you know that I'm a huge fan of the five states of awareness created by copywriting legend Eugene Schwartz.

This states that a prospective buyer, reader, or subscriber starts by being problem unaware, then becomes problem aware, solution unaware, solution aware, and finally, most aware.

Have a look at the diagram below.

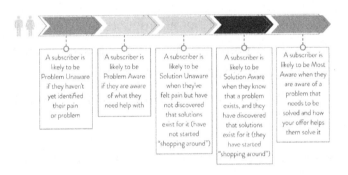

This is one way of thinking about buyer awareness.

Other concepts drop the reader (listener or viewer) into broader phases such as Awareness – Consideration – Decision, or into broad descriptions of Beginner – Intermediate – Advanced.

The terms may vary, but the groupings largely overlap with one another.

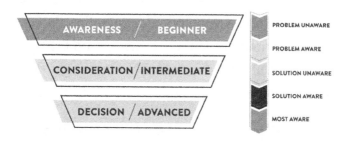

If you're comfortable visualizing your audience using the five states of awareness, use that.

But if you're more comfortable viewing them from an Awareness – Consideration – Decision or Beginner – Intermediate – Advanced angle, use that.

Whichever you use, it doesn't matter.

What's more important is that you understand that the content they need and the questions they have at each of these stages will differ.

What questions do they usually have before saying yes to your offer?

At the **Awareness** stage, some of your readers may have identified a symptom of a potential problem. They may not have identified the real problem but rather are looking for ways to soothe or get rid of their symptoms.

They may also be embarrassed by the questions they have due to their lack of knowledge on this topic.

They are trying to read up on as much material as they can, and the topic is on their radar.

The content here is likely to be centered around the **WHAT** and **WHY.** It should also bring attention to the problem at hand. Create content that shows them everything they could be doing wrong. Pain hits home harder than desire, so get them to sit up and take notice.

- Why should I use [TOPIC] in my life/business?
- What is [TOPIC] about?

- What's the meaning of [BASIC TERMS/ WORDS/JARGON SURROUNDING THE TOPIC]?
- Why I should stop [DOING SOMETHING RELATED TO THE TOPIC]?
- What [MISTAKES RELATED TO THE TOPIC] should I stop making?

At the **Consideration** stage, they have clearly identified their problem and are actively looking for solutions to solve their pain points. You have their attention and you want to throw them a lifeline. How can they solve these pain points or problems?

Create content that helps them solve the mistakes you pointed out earlier. These intermediate readers are actively looking for ways to put this topic to use in their lives. So if you give quick wins and help them implement strategies via step-by-step articles, how-to guides, or tutorials, they are very likely to go on to buy from you.

The content here is likely to be centered around **HOW (application or implementation).**

- How do I do [ONE ASPECT OF THE TOPIC]?
- What tools should I use for [ONE ELEMENT OF THE TOPIC]?
- How can I implement [TOPIC] to do [ONE ASPECT OF THE PROCESS]?

At the **Decision** stage, your reader has a clear understanding of the problem as well as how your solution, framework, or method can fit their needs, their life, or their business. These are the readers who are most primed and ready to buy. They see clearly how the solution can help and want that transformation in their lives.

This transformation can be anything related to the following:

- Cut time
- Get more of a positive result
- Reduce an existing negative result
- Make a task easier
- Get started with something

The content here should be centered around results. Get them to see the light at the other end.

What are the possibilities? Do they know what solutions are out there and how yours is different? Create content to increase their desire to want your solution. When you create a desire for your offer, you make it easy for them to say YES.

- How can I get more of [DESIRED RESULT]?
- What do I need to do to get [DESIRED RESULT]?
- What am I missing out on to get [DESIRED RESULT]?

But how do you know what types of questions to come up with?

This is where you need to consider pain points.

Pain points are thrown around haphazardly, and most people don't know how they are helpful to content.

A pain point is a specific problem that prospective customers at that particular stage are experiencing.

To effectively come up with questions, you need a clear understanding of your audience persona's pain points. I spoke about this in chapter 2 of

The One Hour Content Plan. If you have already mapped out your audience persona—and you have a clear understanding of who this person is—you may be familiar with some of these pain points.

Let's take an example.

In Advanced Web Ranking's *SEO Stats Report 2017*, 65% of over 1,200 online marketers mentioned that link building was the most difficult SEO strategy.[6] Now, if you're creating content for an audience of *online* marketers, which of the following two articles do you think they're more likely to respond to?

1. How to Get Better Results for Your Online Marketing
2. 5 Secret Link-Building Strategies Top Online Marketers Use to Boost SEO

The second article connects the pain point directly to the target audience. People are more likely to click on that.

There are a few different angles from which you can consider pain points:

- Internal

  - What internal factors are causing them stress? For example, fear of not being an expert, English not being their native language, etc.

- External

  - What external factors are causing them stress? For example, the rise in Facebook ad costs, difficulty in getting organic reach, lack of time, etc.

  - What beliefs are your target audience holding on to that are limiting them? For example, I need to be tech savvy to do this, I need to spend a lot of money to start this venture, etc.

You can use any of these angles to work out topic ideas.

What you want to do is list **5–10 questions your audience has at each stage** for each offer you have.

This works out to a potential of ten pieces × three stages of the funnel for each offer. Remember that you are working on the questions for just one audience persona.

STAGE X 10 FRAMEWORK

WHY-WHAT

Awareness /
Beginner Stage /
Bring attention
to the problem

HOW

Consideration /
Intermediate Stage /
Bring interest
in the solution

DESIRE

Decision /
Advanced Stage /
Bring desire for
your solution

Let's apply the STAGE ×10 Framework to our case studies.

CASE STUDY - BEEKEEPING

Bess has a homestead and teaches others how to get started with beekeeping.

OFFER - She has an online class to help beginners learn the basics of beekeeping and honey harvesting.

CORE PROBLEM & SOLUTION - Bess's solution reduces overwhelm that new beekeepers face by equipping them with the steps and tools to take them from zero to having a healthy honey harvest even if they don't have a big budget, are starting from scratch, or have failed at beekeeping before.

WHAT DO THEY NEED TO KNOW BEFORE BEING READY TO BUY - Her ideal customer needs to be aware of the benefits of beekeeping and how it can help their homestead. They also need to know that beekeeping can be simple and doesn't require costly equipment or techniques if they employ the right methods.

WHY-WHAT **Awareness /** **Beginner Stage /** **Bring attention to** **the problem**	10 reasons you should have a beehive in your homestead
	Are you ready for a beehive?
	Beekeeping 101
	Getting started with bees
	Beginner beekeeping mistakes to avoid
HOW **Consideration** **/ Intermediate** **Stage / Bring** **interest in the** **solution**	Where to put your beehive
	How to buy the right bees
	What types of beekeeping equipment to buy
	Costly mistakes in installing your bee colony
DESIRE **Decision /** **Advanced Stage** **/ Bring desire for** **your solution**	How to maximize your honey harvest in 9 steps
	Secrets to hive management
	How this homestead tripled their honey harvest

CASE STUDY - DESIGN SERVICES

Mary runs Spark Design Agency together with a growing number of designers. Her clients are entrepreneurs and small business owners.

OFFER - Her digital agency offers a flat fee unlimited design service.

CORE PROBLEM & SOLUTION - Several business owners face difficulty hiring the right designer. Cost, lack of satisfaction from deliverables, and access are some difficulties faced. Spark offers a solution that is extremely affordable by pairing a dedicated designer with each client.

WHAT DO THEY NEED TO KNOW BEFORE BEING READY TO BUY - Her ideal customer needs to be aware of the benefits of having a designer and how it can help their business. They also need to be convinced of Spark's workflow and solution.

WHY-WHAT Awareness / Beginner Stage / Bring attention to the problem	Design mistakes business owners make and how to correct them
	10 signs you need to hire a designer
	Why hiring a designer is essential for your business growth
	9 reasons small businesses should make graphic design a priority
HOW Consideration / Intermediate Stage / Bring interest in the solution	How do I pick the right designer?
	What tasks can I outsource to a design agency or VA?
	What is your design brand style?
	How to work with your designer for a seamless experience. 10 things you need to discuss beforehand

DESIRE **Decision / Advanced Stage / Bring desire for your solution**	What a match made in design heaven looks like
	What can a graphic designer do for your business?
	How this client brought in 50K in 6 months by outsourcing his design to Spark
	Designs created by Spark in the last 24 hours

CASE STUDY - Visibility & PR

Joan helps female entrepreneurs grow their businesses through strategic public relations.

OFFER - She offers an in-depth DIY course for small business owners who want to start getting noticed through strategic PR.

CORE PROBLEM & SOLUTION - Several business owners neglect PR completely because they don't think it's a necessary part of their strategy. A PR team is also expensive, and they don't think a DIY solution is viable. Joan offers a perfect starter solution and takes someone from nothing to crafting a strategic PR plan for their business even if they don't have a lot of time, are starting from scratch, or have failed at PR before.

WHAT DO THEY NEED TO KNOW BEFORE BEING READY TO BUY - Her ideal customer needs to be aware that PR is a crucial strategy not just for business owners further along in the journey but also for those in the beginner phase as well. They also need to be convinced that a DIY PR solution is a viable option and one that can be successful.

WHY-WHAT **Awareness /** **Beginner Stage /** **Bring attention to** **the problem**	Why PR should be a part of your strategy even if your business is brand new
	7 reasons why you should care about PR even if you're a one-woman shop
	Stop looking like an amateur! Top 10 PR blunders small businesses make and what to learn from them
HOW **Consideration /** **Intermediate Stage** **/ Bring interest in** **the solution**	The beginner's guide to using PR for your small business
	How to figure out what topics to pitch yourself for
	5 PR tools every entrepreneur needs
	6 do-it-yourself PR tips for small businesses
	4 easy ways to get publicity for your business

DESIRE **Decision /** **Advanced Stage** **/ Bring desire for** **your solution**	DIY PR: 10 public relations solutions for small business owners
	Here's how to use PR to attract more clients and boost sales

ACTION

This is where you come in.

You're going to work on the STAGE ×10 Framework for one of your offers (or your affiliate offers) and break it down into questions in this manner. Download the Profitable Content System Playbook for a copy of the STAGE ×10 Template and a swipe file of question prompts. Or simply grab a pen and paper.

Work on the questions for each stage using the question prompts.

Remember to use what you're comfortable with. This could be visualizing your audience using the five states of awareness or viewing them from an Awareness – Consideration – Decision or Beginner – Intermediate – Advanced angle.

But what if you're stuck and can't flesh out any more than five questions per stage?

That's fine!

This is an exercise that you can keep coming back to.

These questions will feed your editorial calendar over time. You're not going to work on them all at once. Keep them in a swipe file, or if you use an editorial calendar like the *CREATE Blog & Editorial Planner*, jot these down under the ideas section.

How exactly do you use these ideas that you just came up with?

This is what we're going to dig into next.

We're heading into the meat of the Profitable Content System.

MEAT & POTATOES — THE HEART OF THE PROFITABLE CONTENT SYSTEM

CHAPTER 2

TRANSFORM YOUR YEAR INTO REVENUE-GENERATING CAMPAIGNS

The first step of the Profitable Content System is learning to think in terms of campaigns.

This might sound scary to you.

If it does, just think of a campaign as a promotion. You're going to pick an offer and build a campaign around it.

A campaign or promotion is nothing more than a coordinated set of content pieces that you create and distribute over a fixed time frame to achieve a specific goal.

Your campaign goals are usually business and marketing goals. These are specific sales and growth targets you're trying to achieve. These are measurable—you can tie an exact number to these goals.

Your goal could be to sell one hundred e-books...

Or increase the number of sign-ups to your membership site by 20%...

Or run a flash sale of your course bundle and double your previous target.

The goal of your campaign will influence everything from who on your email list you're going to send your campaign to, what action you want subscribers to take as well as how you're going to measure the campaign's success. The goal also influences every single content piece you create to support the campaign—anything from your social media posts, emails, blog posts, videos, or infographics.

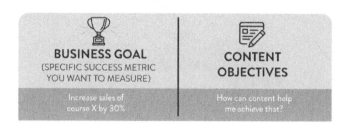

The content pieces you create as part of your campaign are not disjointed content pieces but contribute to a singular goal and have a singular theme around them.

Since this singular message is repeated right through your campaign, it resonates more with your readers and creates incredible momentum for your campaign. It creates an everywhere effect.

When you create content in this way, you take your readers through a journey over the length of your campaign (which runs over a specific time period). It nudges your subscriber toward the end goal of the campaign.

Note: In this book, we're specifically talking about sales, so the campaigns we speak of have a monetary end goal. But this method of content planning can also be used to build authority or brand awareness in a specific area. When I first launched my business, I created a three-month authority push campaign to build authority as a subject matter expert in email marketing. I specifically wrote content pieces to put a stake to my expertise in that topic.

HOW TO INCORPORATE CAMPAIGNS INTO YOUR BUSINESS PLANNING

Learning to structure my year in terms of campaigns was one of my biggest aha moments in business.

Because once you learn how to do this, it's easy to get focused. You will know exactly how each campaign will contribute to your revenue stream. And what content and assets you need to flesh out for each campaign.

That's what planning your year in terms of campaigns or promotions does.

But hang on.

You may be eager to start putting this into action. And you *will* flesh out your campaigns.

Just not right now.

What you need to do first is understand the system.

In the Profitable Content System, there are two different types of campaigns.

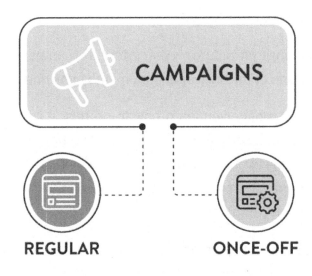

Regular campaigns are those that you usually would run for your core offers. These can be held anytime throughout the year and can be repeated as well.

Once-off campaigns are campaigns that are usually run only once or twice a year. These could be campaigns that are calendar specific. For instance, certain dates in the calendar are important to your business such as birthday-related sales or event-related promotions. These could also be special affiliate promotions that you run for other products. All of these are tied to a specific date or time period in your calendar.

In my own business, I run a yearly campaign called Plan Intensive. This only takes place once a year in October and November.

Now, here are a few questions I want you to think about. Depending on when you picked up this book, you could be looking at a full six months left in the year, a single quarter left in the year, or maybe you picked this book up in November and have a full year ahead of you that you want to plan for.

Pick a suitable time frame.

Start with the next quarter or six months. Prefer to work at a twelve-month stretch? Go ahead!

Answer the following questions based on that time frame.

- What new products do you want to create in this time frame?

- What new services do you want to offer in this time frame?
- Which of your existing offers will you continue to promote in this time frame? For example, are you relaunching any existing offers?

Spread these out over your time frame.

If my time frame is twelve months, this is how my year could look like in terms of campaigns. See the diagram below.

YEAR		
C1	C2	C3
C4	C5	C6
C7	C8	C9
C10	C11	C12

C= CAMPAIGNS

For instance, my project in January could be to release my next book on Amazon.

In February, my project could be to relaunch my signature course.

If you're launching your first product or service and don't have a good grip on what that is yet, I urge you to still put down a tentative launch date. I've seen that putting something down on paper gives you a higher chance of actually considering it and getting it done.

Do you have huge affiliate promotions or sales?

You may know when some of these are. If you do, jot these down as well.

Will you be away during certain months? Then leave those months blank.

Now take a look at your overall calendar. Are certain months too heavy? Move things around till you settle on a workable schedule.

ACTION

Now at this point in time, you may have questions about how long your campaigns should be or how many campaigns you should schedule in a year. We are going to address all of that in the next section.

For now, you just have one single action.

Depending on when in the year you've grabbed this book, I want you to pick a suitable time frame and break it down into revenue-generating campaigns with each campaign promoting an offer you have or intend to have. You can use the template found in the Profitable Content System Playbook at https:// meera.tips/contentplaybook.

CHAPTER 3

HOW TO EXECUTE YOUR REVENUE-GENERATING CAMPAIGNS

Your calendar is now broken down into revenue-generating campaigns or promotions.

But how do you actually execute each campaign?

The first step is to decide what content is going to **feed** your campaign. Remember, your content is going to help you meet the goal you set out for this campaign.

The key question is, how do you know what content to use to promote your offer?

A simple method is to follow the marketing system.

Marketing isn't just about selling or promotion. It's also about attracting and capturing your ideal customers. In a nutshell, marketing is made up of these four activities:

- Attract
- Capture
- Engage
- Convert

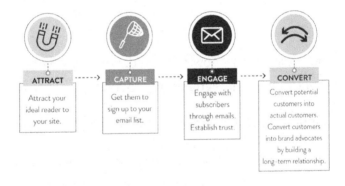

Your campaign needs to have content to cover each of the elements in the marketing system. There are lots of different ideas you can implement but make sure you address these questions so that there are no holes in your campaign.

ATTRACT	CAPTURE	ENGAGE	CONVERT
• Who in your audience do you want to attract? • How are you going to get your content in front of them? • What channels will you use?	• You need to get people on your email list to run a successful campaign. • How are you going get their attention or get them onto your interest or launch list?	• What will you use to engage them? • Will you be using a launch vehicle like a challenge or webinar or video series to help with engagement or conversion?	• What will your sales process be like?

CONTENT PIECES THAT FEED YOUR CAMPAIGN

Here are some examples of content you can use.

Staple content (to attract & capture) addresses audience pain points and raises questions that they need answers to so that they can move through the customer journey. This is usually via your primary content channel—where most people find you and your content (e.g., your podcast, YouTube channel, or blog).

Binge-worthy content (to engage & convert) is an email or video series, workshops and webinars, or a pop-up Facebook group where exclusive content is shared. The characteristic of this content is that it's just that—binge-worthy. These content formats are exclusive and/or only available for a short period of time. These are also likely to be launch vehicles that kick off the start of a launch.

Supplements (to engage) are content pieces that play a support function. They help with brand building and humanizing your brand. These can target any stage right through the customer journey. These are live broadcasts and social media posts.

Regardless of the *type of content* you're creating for your campaign, your content topics are derived from the questions discovered in the STAGE ×10 Framework. So use your STAGE ×10 Framework to flesh out your content topics no matter which *type* they are.

STAPLE (TO ATTRACT & CAPTURE)	BINGE-WORTHY (TO ENGAGE & CONVERT)	SUPPLEMENTS (TO ENGAGE)
Podcasts	Quizzes	Social media posts
YouTube videos	Assessments	Livestreams
Regular newsletters or weekly emails	Video series	Behind the scenes
Blog posts	Workshops	
	Challenges	
	Exclusive lead magnets	
	Webinars	
NOTE: All content is created around the questions discovered in the STAGE ×10 Framework.		

Do you have to include elements from all three verticals in your campaign?

No, you don't!

You don't have to get fancy and do a full-fledged video series or several webinars.

I'm a huge fan of minimum viable. You could simply run an email-only campaign that links to your blog posts and then link to a sales page.

I've run email-only campaigns, kept them really simple and minimum viable, and still made good money.

So don't feel the pressure to add extra elements just because everyone seems to be

doing so. As long as you take an offer and create relevant content pieces depending on what your audience needs to know to be **primed enough** and ready to purchase that offer, you'll be fine!

Let's put this into practice so you can see how this comes together.

Let's say you have a six-week campaign to promote an offer. This could be a service, course, e-book, or even a coaching package.

What could this campaign actually look like?

ATTRACT – CAPTURE – ENGAGE PHASE (PRELAUNCH)

The Attract – Capture – Engage phase of the campaign (or what is the prelaunch campaign) could potentially last 3–4 weeks with the following types of content. What you're doing here is essentially outlining content pieces (blog posts/ videos/podcasts/emails) that will lead up to your launch.

BLOG POSTS (TO ATTRACT & CAPTURE)

Three weeks of blog posts about the topic of the offer. Each blog post can address a question in one stage of the buyer's journey. **Note:** These do not have to be blog posts. These could also be YouTube videos or podcasts.

LEAD MAGNETS OR CONTENT UPGRADES (TO ATTRACT & CAPTURE)

Offer a lead magnet or download about the topic of the offer to your email list. You also want to include content upgrades on each of your blog posts in the campaign as a call to action. This is important because you can tag or identify anyone who clicks on that download from your email list or anyone who chooses to subscribe to that content upgrade and add them to a launch list or a segment. This is the group of people you have identified as being most interested in your offer.

WEEKLY EMAILS (TO ENGAGE)

Four emails on the topic of your offer. You could leave links to your blog posts, but I'm a huge advocate of using your email list as not just an RSS feed or blog post notification channel. Use those same questions that you drafted in the STAGE ×10 Framework. Each email can address a question in one of the stages of the buyer's journey or funnel. You could also pick one point from your blog post, write a short teaser, and then link to the post within your email.

CONVERT PHASE

CONVERT PHASE

The convert phase of the campaign would last 1–2 weeks. There are a few potential ways you could execute your convert phase.

1. You could kick off the convert phase with a launch vehicle such as a webinar or a workshop series. At the end of this event, you could open cart to your offer. This offer could be a coaching package, mastermind, or digital product. The type of product

doesn't matter. The launch vehicle helps to amp up interest and engagement from your audience about the offer. The goal is to **create a desire and need for your offer.**

2. Another method of execution is where your cart opens at the start of your convert phase. This could be via a series of emails with a call to action to check out the sales page.

Now, let's outline a campaign for each of our case studies.

CASE STUDY: Beekeeping **GOAL:** Promote beekeeping course	
Four-Week Campaign	
ATTRACT	• Staple content such as blog posts with a call to action to sign up for content upgrades. • Blog posts will be created around the questions discovered in the STAGE ×10 Framework.

CAPTURE & ENGAGE	• Emails sent right through the length of the campaign. • A download on the topic of offer is given to existing subscribers to create a launch list or interest list.
CONVERT	Cart opens on Week 4 of the campaign.
CONTENT PIECES NEEDED	Blog posts, download, content upgrades, emails

CASE STUDY: Design Service **GOAL:** Promote "Once A Year" birthday promotion of the company with 40% off design plans	
Three-Week Campaign	
ATTRACT & CAPTURE	• Staple content such as blog posts with a call to action to sign up for a guide on stellar examples of existing client designs. • Blog posts will be created around the questions discovered in the STAGE ×10 Framework.

CAPTURE & ENGAGE	• Emails sent right through the length of the campaign. • The download on stellar examples of existing client designs is offered to existing subscribers. • Invite interested subscribers to sign up for an interest list or VIP list.
CONVERT	• Send offer via email to VIP list or interest list. • Invite rest of subscribers to a webinar where the birthday promotion is officially open for sign-up.
CONTENT PIECES NEEDED	Webinar slide deck, blog posts, download, content upgrade, emails

CASE STUDY: Visibility & PR **GOAL:** In-depth DIY course for small business owners who want to start getting noticed through strategic PR
Four-Week Campaign

ATTRACT & CAPTURE	• Staple content such as podcasts with a call to action to sign up for a free 5-day PR Intensive Challenge. • Podcast episodes created around the questions discovered in the STAGE ×10 Framework with a call to action to sign up for the challenge.
ENGAGE	• A pop-up Facebook group with emails sent out right through the 5-day challenge. • 5 challenge emails with supplementary material for challenge-takers. • Webinar held on Day 5 of the challenge.
CONVERT	• Cart opens on Day 5. • Calls to action in emails and webinar to check out the DIY PR course.
CONTENT PIECES NEEDED	Webinar slides, emails, challenge material, podcast episodes

What makes this method effective is that the content you create is directly tied to the topic of your offer.

But I hear you.

Doesn't this seem like a lot of content to create for any campaign?

It depends.

You don't have to create every single piece of content for your campaign from scratch. You can dig into marketing assets you already have.

Marketing assets are elements that are used to carry out any of the four marketing activities outlined above. So these are your content upgrades, lead magnets, blog posts, infographics, sales email deck, and so on.

If you've been in business for some time, you likely have a repository of marketing assets you can dig into. But just like your home is an asset that needs maintenance, repair, and a fresh coat of paint, your marketing assets need to be updated, tweaked, and repackaged.

If your business is new, you probably don't have as many marketing assets built up. Building up marketing assets takes time, but you don't have to create every single piece from scratch. This is where you need to do a content gap analysis to determine what content you already have and what you need to create.

CONTENT GAP ANALYSIS

CONTENT GAP ANALYSIS

How do you do a content gap analysis?

STEP 1

Determine what content the campaign needs. This is what we've been discussing in this chapter.

STEP 2

Determine what content *you already have.* This is where you want to reuse existing content that can be refreshed or tweaked for your campaign.

- Old emails that only a snapshot of your audience have seen
- Videos and ads from previous launches
- Existing posts that can be refreshed
  - Can you go deeper by expanding on the points?
  - Can you go wider by adding additional content to the existing post?
  - Have your viewpoints changed and the post needs an update?
- Content that's relevant but that's not performing
  - Do you have pieces of content that don't generate enough subscribers even with a content upgrade?
  - Maybe the content doesn't get a lot of interest because it needs a better headline?
  - Maybe it needs a different promotion angle?

STEP 3

Determine what new content you need for the campaign.

- Locate gaps in the content for different stages of your funnel or the buyer's journey. What new questions have your audience asked or new pain points that have emerged that you can address with your content? You don't need to use all of these for one campaign. Jot these down and use them as you repeat these campaigns.

You don't have to reinvent the wheel when you're creating content for your campaigns. By doing it this way, you maximize your resources (time and effort).

FAQ 1: Won't my audience notice that I'm repeating emails or blog posts?

You're not repeating the entire email or blog post. You're only repeating the underlying message. At the same time, you're refreshing the content to make it better.

By repeating your messages, they get stronger.

It reinforces your perspective.

You're not watering it down. These messages can be formed out of your story or your journey or your perspective. They can evolve over time. And not everyone in your audience would have seen that piece of content.

FAQ 2: How do I know how much content of each kind to create?

This very much depends on the type of audience you want to attract and serve.

I'm an email marketing strategist and have a course called Profitable Email System™ on how business owners can use email to effectively launch and sell their products. The type of content I create is geared more toward intermediate and advanced readers. Yes, I do have beginner content but not as much and that's intentional.

Remember that beginner content is centered around:

- Why should I use [TOPIC] in my life/business?
- What is [TOPIC] about?

- What's the meaning of [BASIC TERMS/ WORDS/JARGON SURROUNDING TOPIC]?

The audience I want to attract already know of the benefits of an email list. They just don't know how to use it for themselves. I'm not targeting people who are skeptical of email marketing as a solution.

Any content leading up to the launch of my course is focused on intermediate and advanced readers. These are the people who are likely to buy my solution.

Think about the problem that your offer solves or the topic of your offer. Think about who your ideal buyer is likely to be. Then break it up into beginner, intermediate, and advanced.

FAQ 3: How often can I repeat or rerun a campaign?

It depends on how many new eyeballs you have on that offer.

Let's say you ran a campaign for offer X in June and five hundred people went through your campaign. This means you took five hundred people from prelaunch to launch.

If you're repeating the campaign two months later and you're launching offer X again, are there new people besides these five hundred people who you will take through the campaign? Remember that you have to exclude those who have already purchased offer X.

You don't want to exhaust your audience.

Sure there will be people from this earlier group who may be ready to buy right now.

But if the period in between campaign reruns is short, you want to ensure you have fresh new eyeballs on this offer.

This depends on how many targeted subscribers you're able to attract onto your email list in that period of time.

You may have seen others run consecutive launches in short bursts. But dig deeper and you'll see that they run ads. That's how they're able to fill each campaign with a launch list of fresh eyeballs.

This is why it's really important to identify your launch list for each launch. I spoke about this in my book

300 Email Marketing Tips as well. When you have a launch list, you know exactly how many people you've taken from the start to the end of a campaign.

FAQ 4: How long should my prelaunch phase be?

I hate to give you this answer, but IT DEPENDS.

It depends on whether you have content-expert association.

Does your audience consider you an expert or someone they can trust with this topic?

Do they associate that topic with you?

When I launched my book *The One Hour Content Plan*, my audience didn't associate me with the topic of content or content planning. So I did a longer prelaunch phase (Attract – Capture – Engage) of about 4–6 weeks before launching my book.

But if you regularly share content on the topic of your campaign in question, then you may not need an extensive prelaunch campaign. This though is not an excuse to completely skip the Attract – Capture – Engage or prelaunch phase.

There's a ton of benefit in repeating messages.

People forget. People skim content. There will also always be new people in your audience who need to get familiar with your message and point of view when it comes to the topic of your offer.

So never underestimate your prelaunch phase. It can make or break your campaign.

FAQ 5: How do I keep posting content without giving up my "secret sauce"?

This is a valid concern.

The type of content you create should be informed by the type of offer you have.

Have a look at the table below. Use this as a guide to the type of content you should be creating.

If product teaches/is	Give them this type of content
How to do something	Why they should do it
A process (method, step, framework)	Explain why it's important to have that process
Templates/swipe file	Why topic of template/ swipe is important

In the next chapter, I'll walk you step by step through how you can implement everything we've spoken about so far in your own business. You can also download the Campaign Planning Template from the Profitable Content System Playbook at https://meera.tips/contentplaybook.

CHAPTER 4

THE 8-STEP PROFITABLE CONTENT SYSTEM

Let's take a step back and review everything we've covered.

You learned how questions your audience have at each stage of the buyer's journey can fuel your content brainstorming.

You also discovered how you can use campaigns to organize your content so that you attract and lead your targeted audience to appreciate your solution/offer and understand how it can help them.

Now let's review each of the eight steps in the Profitable Content System.

STEP 1 — CHOOSE AN OFFER TO FOCUS ON FOR YOUR CAMPAIGN

Here's an easy way to go about this.

Pick one offer (product or service) to promote every month, once every two months, or every quarter. You can rotate through your offers in this way or lock in specific offers that only make sense at specific time periods.

How frequently you decide to run your campaigns depends on whether

1. You have sufficient time to handhold your audience through the buyer's journey.

2. You have sufficient new people going through your campaign.

Remember that your content has to help your audience

- Recognize they have a problem and show them what this problem is costing them.

- Discover that solutions exist and instill desire for how things could be better if they solved that problem or pain point.

- Understand what they should consider when choosing a solution. At the same time, help them get rid of any false beliefs or objections they have about the solution and its benefits.

- Provide social proof and validate their decision for why your offer is best.

There's no point in pushing yourself to run campaigns every single month if your campaign is not able to do justice to your offer or to your prospective buyer.

STEP 2 — CHOOSE A REVENUE GOAL FOR THE CAMPAIGN

How do you determine a revenue goal for a campaign?

You don't just pluck this number from thin air. You can do this in the following ways:

1. Based on past data

If I know from past experience that I can expect to make 5K on this campaign, that gives me a good gauge of what to expect.

2. Based on the size of your email list and estimated conversation rate

With an email list of one thousand at a 2% conversion rate, I can expect to make twenty sales.

3. Based on your income goals for that campaign

I need Y number of people in my launch list so that at an estimated 3% conversion rate, I will meet my sales target of _____.

You want to work this out for every campaign you run. I have a calculator you can use in the Profitable Content System Playbook so that you can work back on your revenue goals to determine how many people you need on your interest list, or what I call launch list, before you run your campaign.

Remember a launch list or interest list is a group of people you have identified as being interested in your offer. These are the people you handhold right through your campaign from start to finish.

STEP 3 — PLAN YOUR CAMPAIGN

We're using the four-step marketing process here.

There are lots of different ideas you can implement but make sure you address these questions so that there are no holes in your campaign.

ATTRACT	CAPTURE	ENGAGE	CONVERT
• Who in your audience do you want to attract? • How are you going to get your content in front of them? • What channels will you use?	• You need to get people on your email list to run a successful campaign. • How are you going to capture their attention or capture more people onto your interest or launch list?	• What will you use to engage them? • Will you be using a launch vehicle to help with engagement or conversion?	• What will your sales process be like?

STEP 4 — LIST THE SPECIFIC CONTENT PIECES YOU NEED TO CREATE TO SUPPORT YOUR CAMPAIGN

• How many blog posts will you create?

- How many landing pages do you need?
- How many emails do you need to write?
- How many creatives do you need if you're running Facebook Ads?
- What PDFs do you need to create?

Remember that you don't need to recreate every single piece of content from scratch. Do a content gap analysis as I mentioned in the earlier chapter.

STEP 5 — PLOT IN THE EXACT DATES WHEN YOU INTEND TO PUBLISH EACH OF YOUR CONTENT PIECES

STEP 6 — EXECUTE YOUR CAMPAIGN

STEP 7 — REVIEW AND LOCATE GAPS IN YOUR CAMPAIGN

How much revenue did your campaign earn?

Did you meet your sales target?

How did it compare to previous campaigns you ran?

If you didn't meet your revenue target, try to pinpoint why this was so.

Is it because you didn't have enough people going through your campaign to meet the goal?

Or is it because your sales page didn't convert, although you had a healthy click-through rate?

Determine which content pieces and emails performed the best. Identify which content pieces didn't hit the mark as well.

The following will give you clues:

- High impressions, but low conversions
- High open rate, but low click-through rate

STEP 8 — TABLE

What do you need to take note of the next time you run this same campaign?

What ideas do you have for future content pieces? Explore the questions that your audience raised during the campaign.

What can you do to achieve better results?

Let's study a campaign I ran and how this way of planning comes together.

CASE STUDY: PLAN INTENSIVE CHALLENGE 2018

Four-week campaign (pop-up Facebook group and videos were available for another four weeks for those who signed up later)

The goal of this campaign was to promote and sell my two CREATE books on Amazon.

I run this campaign only once a year between October and November. The first time I ran this campaign in 2017, I did a minimum viable campaign. I used blog posts to promote the challenge and used purely email to engage and convert my audience.

The response was amazing, and I knew that the timeline was critical to the success of the campaign. Planning for the new year was top of mind with my audience and this helped drive engagement as well as sign-ups for the campaign. The offer was also relevant to my audience.

I wanted to expand on the success of the campaign. For the 2018 campaign, I wanted to go deeper and engage with my audience. Here's how I executed the campaign.

EXECUTION		
PRELAUNCH	**ATTRACT & CAPTURE**	• Staple content such as blog posts with a call to action to sign up for the Plan Intensive 5-Day Challenge. • - Getting your blog/ biz ready for the new year? Here are 7 MUST-ASK questions for planning success [Intermediate – Consideration] • - 15 lessons on my road to six figures [Intermediate – Consideration] • Four emails in the Attract – Capture – Engage or Prelaunch Phase with a call to action to sign up for the challenge. Two emails also linked to existing blog posts.

		• Images on Pinterest and Facebook to promote the challenge. • Landing page for challenge sign-up.
	ENGAGE	• A pop-up Facebook group with emails sent out right through the 5-day challenge. • Three workshops held through the week teaching the methodology behind the CREATE series of books. • Five challenge emails with supplementary material for challenge-takers.
LAUNCH	**CONVERT**	• Calls to action in emails and workshops to check out the CREATE series of books.

RESULTS		The campaign had a cascading effect and sales for my other books on Amazon saw a significant increase as well. In all, the campaign brought in a combined $14,000 in sales over those two months.

29 Mar 2019	Amazon - (MEERA... Completed	453.85 USD
29 Mar 2019	Amazon - (MEERA... Completed	116.97 USD
29 Mar 2019	Amazon - (MEERA... Completed	58.12 USD
29 Mar 2019	Amazon - (MEERA... Completed	4.05 USD
28 Mar 2019	Amazon - (MEERA... Completed	24.50 USD
28 Mar 2019	Amazon - (MEERA... Completed	6,015.27 USD
28 Feb 2019	Amazon - (MEERA... Completed	130.60 USD
28 Feb 2019	Amazon - (MEERA... Completed	101.32 USD
28 Feb 2019	Amazon - (MEERA... Completed	4.46 USD
28 Feb 2019	Amazon - (MEERA... Completed	622.62 USD
27 Feb 2019	Amazon - (MEERA... Completed	7,194.66 USD
27 Feb 2019	Amazon - (MEERA... Completed	21.03 USD

That's the power of working via campaigns!

When you work in this way, you're looking ahead on your marketing calendar, knowing exactly what you plan to promote and when, and mapping out the exact content pieces you need to help with that promotion.

Every single piece of content in this marketing campaign is aligned and tells the same story because you're clear about the transformation this offer provides and who you're targeting. It also moves people toward appreciating the solution you're offering them.

But even if someone doesn't buy your offer, you're not alienating them. You're still serving them with content that builds your authority and gets them to associate you as someone they can trust when they need help with this topic.

Persistent knocks win in today's online space.

You're building mindshare and staying top of mind so that when people are ready to buy, they come to you.

You now have a system that directly ties content to profit...

That can completely eliminate the blank page phobia...

That can make selling look effortless and guide your ideal customers to appreciate your solutions. But you still may not follow through on this because of holes in your workflow.

This is exactly what you will correct in the next chapter. Let's look at how this system functions at the workflow level.

ACTION

Pick one campaign and start fleshing out ideas on how to execute this campaign by making sure you've considered all aspects of the marketing system: Attract - Capture - Engage - Convert.

Let me know when you're creating your first or next campaign so that I can cheer you on. Tweet me a picture of your campaign planning @meerakothand

CHAPTER 5

HOW TO INCORPORATE THE PROFITABLE CONTENT SYSTEM INTO YOUR WORKFLOW

How do you come up with an efficient workflow so that you're not hustling from one campaign to the next?

Here's how I like to do it.

I like to be one campaign ahead.

So when I'm midway through my current campaign, I look at my calendar and start preparing for the next one. This gives me a buffer of about 3–4 weeks.

But it hasn't always been that way.

As I mentioned earlier, you will build marketing assets that you can reuse over time.

I now have marketing assets I can reuse, so putting a campaign together doesn't take as long as it used to.

You may find yourself struggling when you're starting out with this type of planning.

This is why having a workflow is important.

In my book *The One Hour Content Plan*, I spoke briefly about batching. You may be familiar with this term. It's about doing more of the same at a stretch.

So you don't just write one email or one blog post at a time.

You write three blog posts in one go.

You write six emails or create six branded images in one go.

This saves you time in the long run. It prevents your brain from switching between tasks constantly.

What is critical to this process is your ~~swipe file.~~

A swipe file is filled with content ideas you could use but haven't explored further. Your STAGE ×10 Framework is going to be housed in this swipe file as well. There are lots of tools you can use like Trello, Asana, Google Sheets, or a regular notebook. If you're looking for an editorial planner, consider the CREATE Planner. That's what I use to house my content ideas.

I like to block out the first or last week of the month to batch all the content I need for a campaign.

I already know the campaign I need to work on next. I'm also clear on the goal of that campaign and the offer I'm promoting. So this makes batching a lot easier.

How could this workflow be executed? I'll give you a glimpse into how I do this. Take note that your campaign may not require this many pieces.

WEEK 1 DAY 1

Determine what content pieces my campaign needs.

These could be blog posts, emails, ads, graphics, or landing pages. I'm not creating these yet. I'm just listing down the loose concepts or ideas for each of these segments. Then I lock in specific campaign dates so I know when I need to get the content piece ready by.

Note: This schedule only takes content creation into consideration. It assumes you have your offer and sales page prepared.

CONTENT	TYPE	PUBLISH OR GO LIVE ON
Blog Posts (Dig into STAGE ×10 Framework and swipe file)	Idea 1 rough headline	
	Idea 2 rough headline	
	Idea 3 rough headline	
Email	Prelaunch email 1	
	Prelaunch email 2	
	Prelaunch email 3	
	Reveal email	
	FAQ email	

	Mid-cart bonus email		
	Close cart email		
Ads (Optional)	Open cart text 1		
	Open cart text 2		
	Mid-cart bonus text		
	Close cart text		
Pages (Optional)	Webinar sign-up page		
	Webinar confirmation page		
Downloads	1 lead magnet		
Social Media (Optional)	Campaign Week 1 posts	Long social media post based on an FAQ or a point in an existing blog post	
		Repurposed content from one of your blog posts	

		Reminder to sign up for webinar	
	Campaign Week 2 posts	Repeat above structure	
	Campaign Week 3 posts	Repeat above structure	

WEEK 1 DAY 2

- Finalize blog post headlines. Outline each blog post.

- Create headline variations for each blog post. I do this because Pinterest is a part of my traffic strategy, and I create different pin images for each blog post.

WEEK 1 DAY 3

- Start writing blog posts. I write all my blog posts in a notes document first before moving them onto WordPress.

WEEK 1 DAY 4

- Continue writing blog posts.

WEEK 1 DAY 5

- Write all my emails.

- Finalize topic of launch vehicle (if you're using one).

WEEK 1 DAY 6

- Create necessary landing pages for campaign.

  Note: By the end of the first week, the bulk of your content has already been created. I do work a couple of hours over the weekend, but let's assume you don't and see how this can shift over to the second week.

WEEK 2 DAY 1

- Create launch vehicle content.

- List out all the graphics you need to create.

- **Note:** I currently ship what I need to a designer. But when I was creating my own

- images, I scheduled another day in the week to do them.

BLOG POSTS	Pinterest images (3–4 variations at least per blog post)
	Facebook images
ADS	Open cart creative
	Mid-cart bonus creative
	Close cart creative
PAGES	Webinar mock-up for landing page
SOCIAL MEDIA	Campaign Week 1 posts (2 each)
	Campaign Week 2 posts (2 each)
	Campaign Week 3 posts (2 each)

WEEK 2 DAY 2

- Load emails onto email service provider in drafts.

- Write social media posts.

WEEK 2 DAY 3

- Load blog post text onto WordPress and keep them in drafts.

- Edit your content. Put the finishing touches and upload any images.

WEEK 2 DAYS 4–5

- Create any videos necessary for repurposing.

The only thing left to do is execute your campaign.

This gives you a glimpse into how you can incorporate the Profitable Content System into your workflow.

Does every campaign need to have so many moving parts?

No, it doesn't. You can do email-only minimum viable campaigns which are much easier to handle and are perfect when you're just getting started. This is exactly what I did.

Is working on every campaign as structured and seamless?

Of course not!

There have been campaigns where I only have the content I need for next week ready to go a couple of days ahead of time.

There have also been times where I've had to switch gears and change the campaign I had initially planned for the month to something else. This completely overthrows my scheduling. You may realize a quarter into your year that you are not going to work on certain campaigns at all.

That's ok! Your overview of the year is flexible. And if you do need to make changes, go ahead.

ACTION

Think about how you can incorporate the Profitable Content System into your workflow. What makes sense for your business? If you do plan on batching your content, when in the month could you do so?

SECTION III

CONTENT MAXIMIZERS

In 2017, in a mere 60 seconds online, 500 hours of video on YouTube...

1,440 posts on WordPress...

3.3 million Facebook posts, and

65,972 Instagram photos were uploaded.[7]

People are producing content at an exploding rate today.

Invariably what has happened is that supply has exceeded demand.

In 2014, Mark Schaefer wrote a post called "Content Shock: Why content marketing is not a sustainable strategy."[3] He said that we were at a time when "content supply is exponentially exploding while content demand is flat." Engagement with content has continued to decrease even among the best sites.

Research from BuzzSumo also states that there's a decline in content performance. There are lesser shares and engagement in general.[8]

A shocking 60–70% of marketing content is not used.[9]

Sure, the last stat refers to content in the B2B space, but think about your own content, in your own niche.

Does it seem like getting your content seen is an uphill task—where there's this constant tug and pull between needing to do it and lamenting if it's worth it in the first place?

You already have a fantastic system to tie content to revenue, but how do you ensure people consume your content?

In this section, we'll talk about **maximizing** your content campaigns.

I'll introduce you to a simple repurposing strategy and why most repurposing is setting you up to fail from the very start. I'll also introduce you to the SNAP Recipe where you'll see how you can incorporate content marketing lessons from streaming giants like Netflix.

CHAPTER 6

MINIMUM VIABLE CONTENT REPURPOSING

Most content or how-to articles on repurposing give you about a 50–100 different ways you can repurpose your content.

Yes, it leaves you feeling like you have plenty of options. But when it actually comes down to implementing, you feel lost.

Because those fifty ways don't help very much when you haven't considered the questions that matter.

In this chapter, you'll discover how you can actually use repurposing to maximize or amplify your content campaigns.

So what exactly is repurposing?

It's maximizing the reach of a piece of content through different formats and different channels.

This isn't just sharing the same piece of content on a different channel.

Sure, doing this extends the reach of that piece of content. But repurposing is **offering your existing piece of content in a different format.**

So if your content is primarily text based, you're changing it to audio, video, or images. If your content is primarily video based, you're changing to text, audio, or images.

AUDIO - VIDEO - TEXT - IMAGE-BASED

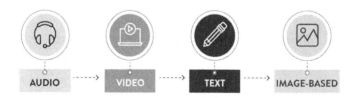

So how can you incorporate a repurposing strategy into the day-to-day of how you do things?

Because if you don't, it will never become a part of your process.

This is what I call **Minimum viable repurposing.**

Here are some questions for you to consider.

You can download them from the Profitable Content System Playbook as well.

1. What is your main content format?

If it's a YouTube channel, your primary format is video. So your repurposing options would fall under the other three content formats: audio, text, and image-based formats.

Likewise, if your primary content format is a podcast (hence audio), you have video, text, and image-based formats to work with.

2. What alternative traffic channels are you active on?

These are not your primary traffic channels but others where you are active or relatively active on. This alternative traffic channel is a platform your audience is active on as well, and it should have given you some results in terms of engagement, reach, or lead generation.

My primary traffic channel is Pinterest. An alternative channel that doesn't get me as much organic reach, but that I'm familiar with and have received decent engagement from my audience, is Facebook.

3. What other content formats do you like to create?

Notice I didn't say *love* to create?

If you love to create a particular format of content, that would most likely be your primary content format.

I love the written medium, which is why I chose a blog.

If you love video, you're likely producing content on YouTube.

This isn't a hard-and-fast rule. So don't panic if you've been creating content in a format that's not aligned with your strengths. But what I've seen from working with several clients is that we all have a natural inclination to pick content channels that are within our strengths or zone of genius.

Consider if this alternative format is also something that your audience likes to consume.

For me, this would be video. I don't *love* it, but I've come to be OK with it.

My audience consume video as well.

Before picking this alternative format, stop for a second and think.

You want to create a frictionless experience with content repurposing.

I mentioned in my book *The One Hour Content Plan* that I don't believe you have to create content in a particular a format because everyone says you should or because it gives you great return on investment.

So if you're going to lock yourself in a room crying at the thought of doing videos or writing a blog post for that matter, I'll say rethink that format again.

It's not off bounds for you but lean in to those that come naturally to you and you'll look at content with enthusiasm—not disdain.

So what can you create that won't make you resent repurposing?

Let's look at some examples.

How could this look for you if written text is currently your main content format?

Here are a couple of options:

WRITTEN TEXT > OTHER CONTENT FORMATS

- Pick the most provocative point from your blog post and create a teaser video with a call to action to read your blog post. Share this on Facebook if this is your alternative platform.

- Create a live video of the main points in the blog post. Embed this video into your blog post and promote it on your alternative platform.

- Create a social media video using an automated tool like Lumen5.

- Transform your blog post into a webinar.

- Have an email that's getting you loads of engagement? Create a short video using the same content and share it on social media. Give a call to action to check out a relevant piece of content.

- Pick one point from your written content and write a long-form social media post. Add emojis, format the post, and give a call to action to check out the blog post.

- Make branded images for Instagram. Pick a point to talk about and link to your blog post.

- Create a slide deck with a cover page and subheads on individual slides. Embed this slide deck into your blog post. This is best used when your alternative platform is LinkedIn or SlideShare.

- Pick info bytes from your blog post and make branded images to share on social media platforms.

- Create an infographic on the main points or to illustrate a data-heavy blog post. Share this on social media with a link to click through to the post.

- Record your blog post and embed the audio file using Libsyn or SoundCloud.

AUDIO > OTHER CONTENT FORMATS

- Pick one point from your audio content and write a long-form social media post. Add emojis, format the post, and give a call to action to check out the audio recording or podcast.

- Pick out quotes from the podcast and create branded images around them.

- Create infographics for data-heavy podcasts.

- Transcribe your audio using a service like Rev or Temi. Offer this as a download for those who prefer to read.

- Create a short paragraph of the main points in your podcast rather than just embedding the podcast file or embedding the transcript.

- Create a slide deck with a cover page and subheads on individual slides. Embed this slide deck into your podcast page. This is best used when your alternative platform is LinkedIn or SlideShare.

- Transform your podcast into a webinar.

- Create a live video of the main points in the podcast. Embed this video into your podcast page.

- Pick the most provocative point from your podcast and create a teaser video with a call to action to listen to your podcast. Share this on Facebook if this is your alternative platform.

VIDEO > OTHER CONTENT FORMATS

- Create a slide deck with a cover page and subheads on individual slides. Embed this slide deck into your podcast page.

- Pick info bytes from your video and make branded images to share on social media platforms.

- Pick one point from your video content and write a long-form social media post. Add emojis, format the post, and give a call to action to check out the video.

- Transcribe your video using a service like Rev or Temi. Offer this as a download for those who prefer to read. Embed captions into your video to help people follow along.

- Create a short paragraph of the main points in your video rather than just embedding the video or embedding the transcript.

This is just scratching the surface of what's possible.

You only want to pick 1–2 repurposing techniques that you can consistently add into your content creation process.

It's not about doing more. It's about your repurposing strategy being frictionless. It's about doubling down and focusing on showing up in one other area where your audience exists and picking a format you're comfortable with.

In the next chapter, we'll talk about one other strategy you can employ to maximize your content and what Netflix has to do with it.

ACTION

Pick one alternative traffic platform you want to use for your repurposing.

Pick one content format you want to use for repurposing.

Identify 1–2 repurposing techniques that will enable you to execute repurposing seamlessly. Is this something that will appeal to your ideal reader as well?

CHAPTER 7

SNAP RECIPE OF CONTENT CREATION

When you think of streaming services, who comes to mind?

Yes, Netflix. And Hulu, Amazon, Disney...

Streaming has changed the way we consume content.

We're all moving away from *owning* content to *accessing* it when and where we want to.

Hate Netflix or don't.

It doesn't matter.

With the amount of content being released on a daily basis, yours needs to thrive.

And there are several lessons you can pick up from these streaming giants and apply to your own content strategy even if you don't have a team.

This is what I call the SNAP Recipe:

Serialization — **N**ovelty — **A**ctivation — **P**ersonalization

Here are a couple of ways you can incorporate SNAP into your content strategy.

1. SERIALIZATION

Netflix made binging popular.

Rather than releasing one episode a week and building hype and anticipation, it releases multiple episodes in short bursts.

This gives the audience control over how they watch the content they like.

Netflix has also resisted ads that take away from the content experience.

Netflix bends the rules because it understands its users' behavior. It has built a model that delights and rewards extremely engaged viewers.

This is similar to the rapid release strategy in the self-publishing space. Several authors have found success from releasing books one after the other in quick succession. This rapid release strategy allows them to capitalize on their audience's attention when they have it.

How can you apply this to your own campaigns?

- **Have one-off content campaigns**
- These are campaigns that you only add into your calendar every quarter or once every six months. This makes it exclusive, increases attention, and makes it binge-worthy especially if your audience knows the content's going to disappear.
- For example, I only run my Plan Intensive challenge once a year, and the videos and content are available for only a few weeks before I take them down.

- **Create an event**
- Create an event around your content creation and give that event a purpose or theme. I've done this with my email challenges. Because these happen over a fixed duration and only a few times a year, it increases excitement and audience engagement.

Meera Kothand
Admin · January 23

WELCOME TO THE CHALLENGE!
Watch this quick video first!
If you haven't signed up for the challenge, you can do so here:
https://meera.email/challenge... See More

55   27 Comments

- **Have seasonal podcast episodes on a theme**
- Sure, there are pros and cons to having seasonal podcasts as there are with any strategy. But having it on a seasonal basis allows you to work

around lower content consumption periods like Christmas or summer. There are ebbs and flows in every industry. This could also build anticipation for the show's return and allow you to cover topics more thoroughly.

2. NOVELTY

Netflix has staple content that it curates from other networks like *Gilmore Girls* or *How to Get Away with Murder*. But it also creates content that other companies don't have via its original series like *Black Mirror*, *Orange Is the New Black*, *Stranger Things*, and more.

How you can apply this:

In my book *But I'm Not an Expert!* I shared that valuable content is content that has three defining attributes.

It kills sacred cows - This is content that proves wrong popular myths and beliefs that are immune to criticism or questions.

It fills an opportunity gap - It addresses frequently asked questions that the competition hasn't adequately addressed. It also provides another viewpoint or angle in answering these questions.

It has a clearly identifiable point of view - This is content that takes a stance about the topics and problems in your niche. These views could be polarizing to a certain extent, but that's what makes people decide whether to follow you and continue to read your content. These are what opinion posts are made up of.

Do research on your competitors and their content.

What kind of content are they providing and where do they lack? How can you present your content in a novel way?

One example of this is the Candid Confidence project[10] by Tara McMullin, founder & host of *What Works*. The project delivered essays, interviews, and conversations over Instagram exploring the many ways entrepreneurs face insecurity and level up.

3. ACTIVATE YOUR AUDIENCE

Netflix knows its audience loves humorous content that they can share with their friends. So it often posts funny GIFs, memes, and videos on its social media accounts. It also leans in to the feelings their audience have about specific shows and posts content that boosts audience engagement.

How you can apply this:

. **Build marketing into your campaigns**
. Get your audience to be a part of the conversation. Get them to share or tweet as they are consuming your content. Pat Flynn

of **Smart Passive Income** did it with his book **Will It Fly?** where he asked his audience to send him specific videos and pictures of them reading his book. This content becomes a part of your marketing content as well.

- **Build a scream team or launch team for your campaigns**
- I do this often for book launches. Bring together a group of people who are perfect audiences for your campaigns. Get their help to generate buzz around your campaign via social media or do live videos for their audiences. This is how you build word of mouth for your campaigns.
- You could also make this "application only." You can have this scream team work with you for six months or a year to help promote your campaigns. They are most likely your brand advocates and raving fans. Incentivize them with discounts, early access passes, or behind-the-scenes content.
- **Release shorter bites of content**
- I don't believe in every day content creation with no intent, but smaller bites of content in

the style of lives, stories, or social media posts can supplement your existing content and humanize your brand.

4. PERSONALIZATION

Netflix's algorithms and data collection methods allow it to recommend specific shows based on what its consumers have already watched. It also utilizes data in its promotion methods. For instance, ten different trailers were created for promoting season two of *House of Cards* based on users' age, gender, and viewing preferences. If the Netflix user was female, she might get a trailer that is focused on the female characters in the show.

How you can apply this:

- **Put your audience in the driver's seat**

   Offer them different types of content they may be interested in. This could be via "choose your journey" email sequences or one-click sign-ups of other free content once they've completed their current ones.

   You could also set up quizzes via tools like ManyChat, Thrive Quiz Builder, or Interact.

Direct your audience to personalized content based on their responses to your questions. Have a look at a quiz I did for my audience here: https://meera.email/quiz.

. **Do simple A/B testing**

While you may not have access to sophisticated algorithms and tools like the big companies do, you can still employ simple A/B testing of landing pages and headlines using tools like Thrive Optimize.

Use Facebook polls or check your Google Analytics to see which content has been performing well. What is your audience sharing now?

The Profitable Content System itself is structured in a way that it gets you to think about and apply several elements of SNAP into your campaigns.

ACTION

How can you implement the SNAP Recipe into your content creation? What ideas come to mind?

CONCLUSION

Content marketing used to be a good strategy to build your brand and business.

The belief was that the more content you produced...

The more you attracted your ideal audience...

The greater the amount of traffic you drove to your site...

And the more people you'd convert to clients and buyers.

When content marketing became a buzz word, people started producing content (still do) at an exploding rate.

It's no longer feasible to just create content because the chances of your content actually getting seen, heard, or read are getting smaller. You need to be able to justify every single infographic or email or social media post you create.

In the last few chapters, you discovered how to organize your content based around your products and services. I hope you can see now that there is a direct link between content and sales and how your audience use content to inform their buying decision.

You also have a workflow for how to execute a profit-driven content plan without burnout and to maximize your efforts without random content distractions.

Before you create a single piece of content, ask yourself if you'll be driving people to your website that have the ability and willingness to buy from you. Because if you don't, you'll struggle to turn those visitors into leads, sales, and profits.

Stop writing content for yourself or because someone else is doing something similar and start writing for people who want to buy from you.

When you create hard-to-resist campaigns around your products and services, it becomes insanely easy to go from endless hustling to easily booked or sold out.

You can show up and sell without feeling like you're spamming people...without feeling pressured to pitch in a sneaky, salesy way.

I hope you give the Profitable Content System a try.

Remember to download your bonuses at <u>https://meera.tips/contentplaybook.</u>

Good luck and thank you for sharing your work with the world!

THANK YOU FOR READING

I hope you enjoyed reading this book.

I really appreciate your feedback, and I love hearing what you have to say.

Could you leave me a review on Amazon letting me know what you thought of the book?

Thank you so much! If you want to get in touch, come find me here at my slice of the internet: https://www.meerakothand.com.

Meera

ABOUT THE AUTHOR

Meera is an email marketing strategist and 3×
Amazon best-selling author of the books *The
One Hour Content Plan*, *But I'm Not an Expert!*
& *Your First 100*. She is also the publisher of
MeeraKothand.Com, an award-winning site listed
as one of the 100 Best Sites for Solopreneurs
in 2017 and 2018, and the popular CREATE
Planners. Using her unique Profitable Email
System™ and ADDICTED™ Business Framework,
she makes powerful marketing strategies simple
and relatable so that small business owners can
build a tribe that's addicted to their zone of genius.

Other Books on Amazon

RESOURCES

1. Brian Carroll, *Lead Generation for the Complex Sale* (New York: McGraw-Hill Education, 2006), https://www.amazon.com/Lead-Generation-Complex-Sale-Quantity/dp/0071458972.

2. Michael Barnett, "New year's resolutions required for content marketers," *Marketing Week*, January 6, 2015,

https://www.marketingweek.com/2015/01/06/new-years-resolutions-required-for-content-marketers/.

3. Mark Schaefer, "Content Shock: Why content marketing is not a sustainable strategy," *Businesses Grow*, January 6, 2014, https://businessesgrow.com/2014/01/06/content-shock/.

4. "Zero Moment of Truth (ZMOT)," *Think with Google*, accessed September 4, 2019,

https://www.thinkwithgoogle.com/marketing-resources/micro-moments/zero-moment-truth/.

5. Jim Lecinski, *Winning the Zero Moment of Truth* (Chicago: Google Inc, 2011), 10, https://www.thinkwithgoogle.com/marketing-resources/micro-moments/2011-winning-zmot-ebook/.

6. Advanced Web Ranking, *SEO Stats Report 2017*, https://www.advancedwebranking.com/seo-stats-report-2017.html.

7. Douglas Karr, "How Much Content is Produced Online in 60 Seconds?" *Martech*, June 6, 2017, https://martech.zone/how-much-content-online-60-sec/.

8. Steve Rayson, "50% of Content Gets 8 Shares Or Less: Why Content Fails And How To Fix It," *BuzzSumo*, November 10, 2015, https://buzzsumo.com/blog/50-of-content-gets-8-shares-or-less-why-content-fails-and-how-to-fix-it/.

9. Jessica Lillian, "Summit 2013 Highlights: Inciting a B-to-B Content Revolution,"

SiriusDecisions, May 9, 2013, https://www. siriusdecisions.com/blog/summit-2013- highlights-inciting-a-btob-content-revolution.

10. Candid Confidence project, http:// explorewhatworks.com/confidence/.

Buyers Journey :

P.36
P.38

Become Aware (why, / what)

Consider / Evaluate (How)

Decide to Purchase (Desire)

★ Work on the questions

Marketing is made up of 4 activities

P.61

- Attract ⎫ staple
- Capture ⎭ content
- Engage
- Convert

How to keep posting without giving up

My "secret sauce" .

    P. 80

Direct audience to personalize 1
content based on their responses
to your questions   P.130

Lumens → videos

Personalization